What's for lunch?

chocolate

D1088589

Library of Congress Cataloging-in-Publication Data
Llewellyn, Claire.
    Chocolate / Claire Llewellyn.
    p.   cm. -- (What's for lunch?)
    Includes Index.
    Summary: Presents facts about the cocoa bean, including how it is grown,
    harvested, and marketed and finally turned into a variety of chocolate products.
    ISBN 0-516-20837-3
    1. Cocoa beans --Juvenile literature. 2. Chocolate--Juvenile
literature. [1. Cacao beans. 2. Chocolate] I. Title. II. Series.
Llewellyn, Claire. What's for Lunch?
SB267. L54 1998   97-34943
641.3'374--dc21   CIP
                                                    AC

© 1998 Franklin Watts
96 Leonard Street
London
EC2A 4RH

First American edition 1998 by
Franklin Watts
A Division of Grolier Publishing
Sherman Turnpike
Danbury, CT 06816

ISBN 0-516-20837-3

Editor: Samantha Armstrong
Series Designer: Kirstie Billingham
Designer: Kelly Flynn
Consultant: Cadbury Ltd.
Reading Consultant: Prue Goodwin, Reading and Language
Information Centre, Reading.

Printed in Hong Kong

What's for lunch?

Chocolate

Claire Llewellyn

CHILDREN'S PRESS®

A Division of Grolier Publishing

NEW YORK • LONDON • HONG KONG • SYDNEY
DANBURY, CONNECTICUT

NORTH BAY
SEP 1 1999
PUBLIC LIBRARY
DISCARDED

J
X
641.3
Lle

A 4-8

Today we are having chocolate cake.
It is a special treat.
Chocolate contains **sugar** and **fat**
and gives us **energy**.

Chocolate is made from **cocoa beans,**
which grow on cocoa trees.
The trees grow in warm,
wet parts of the world,
on large farms called **plantations**.

Tiny flowers grow on the trees.
After a few weeks,
the flowers develop into **pods**.
Cocoa beans grow inside the pods.
There are thirty to forty beans
inside each pod.

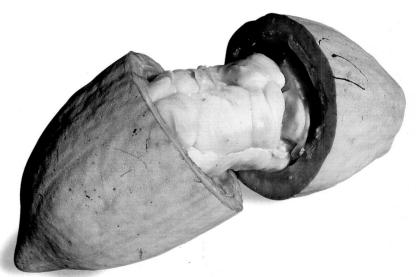

Farmers take great care
of the **crop**.
They spray the trees
with **insecticide**
to protect them from
pests and **diseases**.
Sometimes they give
them extra water.

After about six months,
when the pods have turned
a reddish-orange color,
the farmers use knives to cut them down.
They split the pods open
and remove the cocoa beans.

The beans are spread out
to dry in the sun for a week
and are turned regularly.
This makes sure they
don't become **moldy**.
Then the dried beans
are put into sacks
and taken to factories.

At the factories,
the sacks of beans are cut open
and any insects or bits of cocoa plant
are picked out.

The beans are cleaned and **roasted**
to bring out their flavor.
Then the beans are **ground** until they
become a liquid, fatty cream
called **cocoa mass**.

Sometimes all the liquid
is squeezed out of the cocoa mass
until it leaves a solid block of cocoa
that can be ground into powder.
Cocoa powder is used
to make chocolate drinks.
Or it can add a chocolate flavor
to sauces, cakes, and ice cream.

To make chocolate for candy,
the cocoa mass is mixed with milk and sugar.
Specially trained **tasters** check the chocolate
to make sure that it looks, tastes,
and feels just right.

The chocolate is poured into **molds** and chilled until it is hard. Sometimes, nuts, **raisins,** or puffed rice are mixed in with the chocolate.

NORTH BAY PUBLIC LIBRARY SEP 1 - 1999

Bars of chocolate are wrapped in **foil**
to keep them fresh.
Then they are delivered to stores,
where they are ready for people to buy.

Chocolate can be made into
all sorts of different shapes.

Most people love chocolate. It is sweet and delicious and always a special treat.

NORTH BAY PUBLIC LIBRARY SEP 1 - 1999

Glossary

cocoa beans the seeds of the cocoa tree

cocoa mass the cream that comes from ground cocoa beans

cocoa powder powdered chocolate used to make drinks or add a chocolate flavor to sauces, cakes, and ice cream

crop what farmers grow in their fields

disease something that attacks plants or animals

energy the strength to work and play

fat something found in food that gives us energy

foil metal that is made into thin sheets and used to wrap food to keep it fresh

ground crushed into small bits

insecticide something that kills insects

mold	a tray with a special shape, that when liquid chocolate is poured into it, the cooled chocolate takes on the shape of the mold
moldy	to be covered with growth and bad to eat
pest	an animal such as a beetle or fly that spoils or destroys crops
plantation	a large piece of land used to grow just one type of plant, such as cocoa trees
pod	the part of a plant that grows on the cocoa tree and contains the cocoa beans
raisin	a sweet grape that has been dried
roasted	cooked in an oven
sugar	something that is added to food and drink to make them taste sweet
tasters	people who eat small amounts of chocolate to make sure it tastes just right

Index

cocoa beans 6, 9, 12, 14, 17, 18

cocoa mass 18, 20

cocoa powder 20

cocoa trees 6, 9, 11

crop 11

diseases 11

insecticide 11

molds 25

pests 11

plantations 6

pods 9, 12

tasters 22

Picture credits: Cadbury Ltd. 12. 16-17, 19, 26; Holt Studios International: 6-7, 8, 9, 10, 11, 14 (all Nigel Cattlin); Panos Pictures (Crispin Hughes) 14-15; Robert Harding 13; Rowntree-Nestle Ltd. 24; Zefa-Bramaz 23; Steve Shott cover; All other photographs Tim Ridley, Wells Street Studios, London.
With thanks to Scarlett Carney and Thomas Ong.